HoD

Please renew or return items by the date
shown on your receipt

www.hertfordshire.gov.uk/libraries

Renewals and enquiries: 0300 123 4049

Textphone for hearing or 0300 123 4041
speech impaired users:

Hertfordshire

L32 11.16

FREE AUDIO
website and app
www.dkefe.com

D1347540

Author

Barbara MacKay is an experienced English-language teacher and author. She has written for major English-language publishers including Oxford University Press and Macmillan Education.

Course consultant

Tim Bowen has taught English and trained teachers in more than 30 countries worldwide. He is the co-author of works on pronunciation teaching and language-teaching methodology, and author of numerous books for English-language teachers. He is currently a freelance materials writer, editor, and translator. He is a member of the Chartered Institute of Linguists.

Language consultant

Professor Susan Barduhn is an experienced English-language teacher, teacher trainer, and author, who has contributed to numerous publications. In addition to directing English-language courses in at least four different continents, she has been President of the International Association of Teachers of English as a Foreign Language, and an adviser to the British Council and the US State Department. She is currently a Professor at the School of International Training in Vermont, USA.

ENGLISH
FOR EVERYONE

PRACTICE BOOK

LEVEL ❸ INTERMEDIATE

DK India
Senior Editors Vineetha Mokkil, Anita Kakar
Senior Art Editor Chhaya Sajwan
Project Editor Antara Moitra
Editors Agnibesh Das, Nisha Shaw, Seetha Natesh
Art Editors Namita, Heena Sharma, Sukriti Sobti,
Shipra Jain, Aanchal Singhal
Assistant Editors Ira Pundeer, Ateendriya Gupta,
Sneha Sunder Benjamin, Ankita Yadav
Assistant Art Editors Roshni Kapur,
Meenal Goel, Priyansha Tuli
Illustrators Ivy Roy, Arun Pottirayil, Bharti Karakoti, Rahul Kumar
Picture Researcher Deepak Negi
Managing Editor Pakshalika Jayaprakash
Managing Art Editor Arunesh Talapatra
Production Manager Pankaj Sharma
Pre-production Manager Balwant Singh
Senior DTP Designer Vishal Bhatia, Neeraj Bhatia
DTP Designer Sachin Gupta
Jacket Designer Surabhi Wadhwa
Managing Jackets Editor Saloni Singh
Senior DTP Designer (jackets) Harish Aggarwal

DK UK
Editorial Assistants Jessica Cawthra, Sarah Edwards
Illustrators Edwood Burn, Denise Joos, Michael Parkin,
Jemma Westing
Audio Producer Liz Hammond
Managing Editor Daniel Mills
Managing Art Editor Anna Hall
Project Manager Christine Stroyan
Jacket Designer Natalie Godwin
Jacket Editor Claire Gell
Jacket Design Development Manager Sophia MTT
Producer, Pre-Production Luca Frassinetti
Producer Mary Slater
Publisher Andrew Macintyre
Art Director Karen Self
Publishing Director Jonathan Metcalf

First published in Great Britain in 2016 by
Dorling Kindersley Limited
80 Strand, London, WC2R 0RL

Copyright © 2016 Dorling Kindersley Limited
A Penguin Random House Company
10 8 6 4 2 3 5 7 9
012–290005–Jun/2016

A CIP catalogue record for this book
is available from the British Library.
ISBN: 978-0-2412-4352-7

Printed and bound in China

All images © Dorling Kindersley Limited
For further information see: www.dkimages.com

A WORLD OF IDEAS:
SEE ALL THERE IS TO KNOW

www.dk.com

Contents

How the course works

English for Everyone is designed for people who want to teach themselves the English language. Like all language courses, it covers the core skills: grammar, vocabulary, pronunciation, listening, speaking, reading, and writing. Unlike in other courses, the skills are taught and practiced as visually as possible, using images and graphics to help you understand and remember. The practice book is packed with exercises designed to reinforce the lessons you have learned in the course book. Work through the units in order, making full use of the audio available on the website and app.

COURSE BOOK

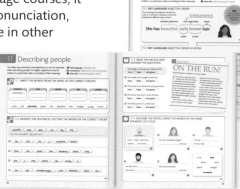

PRACTICE BOOK

Unit number The book is divided into units. Each practice book unit tests the language taught in the course book unit with the same number.

Practice points Every unit begins with a summary of the key practice points.

26 Activities in progress

Use the present perfect continuous to talk about ongoing activities in the past. Use "for" and "since" to talk about the length or starting point of an activity.

New language Present perfect continuous
Aa Vocabulary Home improvements
New skill Talking about activities in the past

Modules Each unit is broken down into modules, which should be done in order. You can take a break from learning after completing any module.

26.1 FILL IN THE GAPS BY PUTTING THE VERBS IN THE PRESENT PERFECT CONTINUOUS TENSE

Fatima _____ *has been shopping* _____ (shop) for clothes all day.

① Nathan _____ (read) a book in the back yard.

② I _____ (cook) breakfast in the kitchen.

③ Mike _____ (play) tennis with his friends.

④ Ted and John _____ (watch) TV all evening.

⑤ Mrs. Roberts _____ (paint) the house this weekend.

26.2 FILL IN THE GAPS USING "FOR" OR "SINCE"

I've been waiting _____ *for* _____ 20 minutes.

① He has been fishing _____ 3:30pm.
② We've been learning Spanish _____ six weeks.
③ Ruth has been cooking _____ a long time.
④ You've been decorating _____ March 8.
⑤ I've been driving _____ 11:45am.

⑥ He's been teaching science _____ 2012.
⑦ She's been watching TV _____ two hours.
⑧ I've been learning to dance _____ two weeks.
⑨ Alan has been tiling the floor _____ Monday.
⑩ It has been snowing _____ 10 days.
⑪ I've been working at home _____ last April.

26.3 READ THE EMAIL AND NUMBER TH... ORDER THEY ARE DESCRIBED

Ⓐ ☐   Ⓑ 1   Ⓒ ☐

Ⓓ ☐   Ⓔ ☐   Ⓕ ☐

26.4 LISTEN TO THE AUDIO AND WRITE... HAS BEEN GOING ON

since last weekend   ①

③   ④

Vocabulary Throughout the book, vocabulary pages test your memory of key English words and phrases taught in the course book.

Visual practice Images and graphics offer visual cues to help fix the most useful and important English words in your memory.

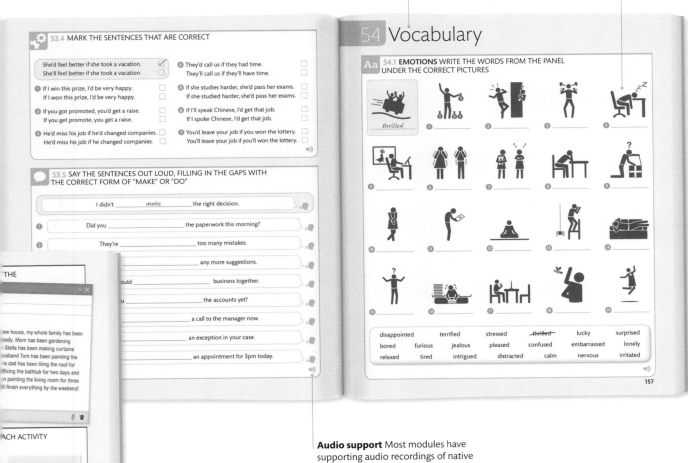

53.4 MARK THE SENTENCES THAT ARE CORRECT

She'd feel better if she took a vacation. ☑	④ They'd call us if they had time. ☐
She'll feel better if she took a vacation. ☐	They'll call us if they'll have time. ☐
① If I win this prize, I'd be very happy. ☐	⑤ If she studies harder, she'd pass her exams. ☐
If I won this prize, I'd be very happy. ☐	If she studied harder, she'd pass her exams. ☐
② If you got promoted, you'd get a raise. ☐	⑥ If I'll speak Chinese, I'd get that job. ☐
If you get promote, you get a raise. ☐	If I spoke Chinese, I'd get that job. ☐
③ He'd miss his job if he'd changed companies. ☐	⑦ You'd leave your job if you won the lottery. ☐
He'd miss his job if he changed companies. ☐	You'll leave your job if you'll won the lottery. ☐

53.5 SAY THE SENTENCES OUT LOUD, FILLING IN THE GAPS WITH THE CORRECT FORM OF "MAKE" OR "DO"

I didn't ___ *make* ___ the right decision.

① Did you ___ the paperwork this morning?

② They're ___ too many mistakes.

___ any more suggestions.

...ould ___ business together.

...u ___ the accounts yet?

___ a call to the manager now.

___ an exception in your case.

___ an appointment for 3pm today.

ew house, my whole family has been
...ady. Mom has been gardening
...Stella has been making curtains
...usband Tom has been painting the
...is dad has been tiling the roof for
...fixing the bathtub for two days and
...n painting the living room for three
...ll finish everything by the weekend!

...ACH ACTIVITY

75

54 Vocabulary

Aa 54.1 **EMOTIONS** WRITE THE WORDS FROM THE PANEL UNDER THE CORRECT PICTURES

thrilled

disappointed	terrified	stressed	~~thrilled~~	lucky	surprised
bored	furious	jealous	pleased	confused	embarrassed	lonely
relaxed	tired	intrigued	distracted	calm	nervous	irritated

157

Audio support Most modules have supporting audio recordings of native English speakers to help you improve your speaking and listening skills.

FREE AUDIO
website and app
www.dkefe.com

Practice modules

Each exercise is carefully graded to drill and test the language taught in the corresponding course book units. Working through the exercises alongside the course book will help you remember what you have learned and become more fluent. Every exercise is introduced with a symbol to indicate which skill is being practiced.

 GRAMMAR
Apply new language rules in different contexts.

 READING
Examine target language in real-life English contexts.

 LISTENING
Test your understanding of spoken English.

VOCABULARY
Cement your understanding of key vocabulary.

 SPEAKING
Compare your spoken English to model audio recordings.

Module number Every module is identified with a unique number, so you can easily locate answers and related audio.

Exercise instruction Every exercise is introduced with a brief instruction, telling you what you need to do.

Sample answer The first question of each exercise is answered for you, to help make the task easy to understand.

Space for writing You are encouraged to write your answers in the book for future reference.

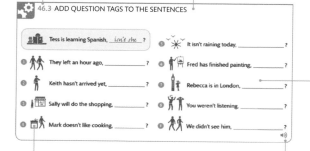

Supporting graphics Visual cues are given to help you understand the exercises.

Supporting audio This symbol shows that the answers to the exercise are available as audio tracks. Listen to them after completing the exercise.

Listening exercise This symbol indicates that you should listen to an audio track in order to answer the questions in the exercise.

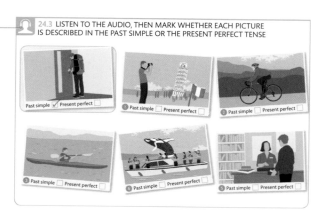

Speaking exercise This symbol indicates that you should say your answers out loud, then compare them to model recordings included in your audio files.

Audio

English for Everyone features extensive supporting audio materials. You are encouraged to use them as much as you can, to improve your understanding of spoken English, and to make your own accent and pronunciation more natural. Each file can be played, paused, and repeated as often as you like, until you are confident you understand what has been said.

LISTENING EXERCISES
This symbol indicates that you should listen to an audio track in order to answer the questions in the exercise.

SUPPORTING AUDIO
This symbol indicates that extra audio material is available for you to listen to after completing the module.

FREE AUDIO
website and app
www.dkefe.com

Answers

An answers section at the back of the book lists the correct answers for every exercise. Turn to these pages whenever you finish a module and compare your answers with the samples provided, to see how well you have understood each teaching point.

30

30.1 ◀))
1. **The supermarket** is open on Sundays.
2. I don't like studying for **exams**.
3. **The last movie** I saw was really good.
4. It always rains during **vacations**.
5. I go to **work** by train.
6. He likes reading **the newspaper**.
7. Adam works in **the local hospital**.
8. I hate shopping for **food**.
9. **Fries** aren't good for you.
10. I like **the photo** on your desk.
11. **The boss** is happy with my work.
12. Karen has lots of **shoes**.
13. I like going to **the movie theater**.
14. **The suit** is expensive.
15. I'm going to **the bank** to get a loan.
16. Dan hates **fruit**.
17. I will spend **the money** I got from my aunt.
18. **The car** isn't working.
19. I love **dancing**.

> **Answers** Find the answers to every exercise printed at the back of the book.

30.2 ◀))
1. Where are the keys for the shed?
2. We love playing sports.
3. The dishwasher isn't working.
4. Here's the book I borrowed.
5. The last movie I saw was terrible.
6. That woman has lots of cats.
7. When do you go back to work?
8. The person outside is my uncle.
9. Look at the tablet I bought yesterday.
10. Dentists earn a lot of money.
11. I'm going to the post office.

> **Audio** This symbol indicates that the answers can also be listened to.

30.3
Hi Richard,
I've gone to **the post office** to send back **the parcel** that came **last week**. I don't want **the shoes** because they're too big for me. When I've done that, I'll go to **the supermarket** and buy **potatoes** so we can make fries for dinner. Can you check if **the cat** has eaten **the food** I left her? She wasn't feeling very well yesterday.
Thanks!
Carla

> **Exercise numbers** Match these numbers to the unique identifier at the top-left corner of each exercise.

30.4
1. The campsite is in the south of France.
2. She has to clean the tents.
3. She hates doing the cleaning.
4. They play games and go to the beach.
5. She buys wine from the local vineyard.

01 Making conversation

In spoken English, you might hear small questions added to the ends of sentences. These are called question tags, and they are used to invite someone to agree with you.

⚙ **New language** Question tags
Aa Vocabulary Introductions and greetings
New skill Making conversation

1.1 MATCH THE BEGINNINGS OF THE SENTENCES TO THE CORRECT ENDINGS

John is a great friend, ——————→ isn't he?

1 Mom isn't at work today,   isn't it?

2 You're a flamenco dancer,   aren't they?

3 I'm not sitting in your chair,   aren't you?

4 This article is very interesting,   isn't he?

5 They're from Beijing,   is she?

          am I?

◀))

1.2 MARK THE SENTENCES THAT ARE CORRECT

Her dress is beautiful, aren't I? ☐
Her dress is beautiful, isn't it? ☑

1 You're hungry, aren't you? ☐
   You're hungry, aren't I? ☐

2 She is Chris's boss, isn't he? ☐
   She is Chris's boss, isn't she? ☐

3 They're from Florida, aren't they? ☐
   They're from Florida, isn't they? ☐

4 It's warm today, is she? ☐
   It's warm today, isn't it? ☐

5 You're not tired, aren't I? ☐
   You're not tired, are you? ☐

6 We're from the same town, are they? ☐
   We're from the same town, aren't we? ☐

7 They're late, aren't they? ☐
   They're late, are you? ☐

8 Saira's sister is here, are they? ☐
   Saira's sister is here, isn't she? ☐

9 You're from the US, aren't you? ☐
   You're from the US, is it? ☐

◀))

1.3 SAY THE SENTENCES OUT LOUD, ADDING QUESTION TAGS

The food is delicious, _____*isn't it?*_____

1 The music is very loud, _____

2 You're not from here, _____

3 Tim is a great dancer, _____

4 Fiona isn't here, _____

5 The venue is lovely, _____

6 I'm not late, _____

7 They are dancing, _____

8 The band is great, _____

9 You're having a good time, _____

10 It isn't warm today, _____

11 I'm in your class, _____

12 He isn't 30, _____

13 You aren't waiting, _____

14 This film is boring, _____

15 They're playing tennis, _____

16 We aren't early, _____

17 She's beautiful, _____

18 You aren't from Boston, _____

19 He isn't outside, _____

20 They're watching TV, _____

21 You aren't hurt, _____

1.4 FILL IN THE GAPS, ADDING QUESTION TAGS

It's very cold, _____*isn't it*_____ ?

1 You're Sarah, _____ ?

2 You're Sally's friend, _____ ?

3 Fatima is funny, _____ ?

4 The food is delicious, _____ ?

5 Dev and Jai are twins, _____ ?

6 You're not leaving now, _____ ?

7 I'm not boring you, _____ ?

8 The boss isn't here, _____ ?

9 I'm late, _____ ?

10 You've just woken up, _____ ?

11 You can't see it, _____ ?

12 He's getting old, _____ ?

13 They're not studying, _____ ?

1.5 LISTEN TO THE AUDIO AND ANSWER THE QUESTIONS

Helena is at a party organized by her friend Danny's boss.

Danny and Helena are at a work party.
True ☑ **False** ☐

1 Danny introduces Helena to his boss.
True ☐ **False** ☐

2 Rachel and Chris are Danny's friends.
True ☐ **False** ☐

3 Rachel and Chris work in different offices.
True ☐ **False** ☐

4 Rachel knows nothing about Helena.
True ☐ **False** ☐

5 Helena likes the band.
True ☐ **False** ☐

6 Helena thinks the music is a bit loud.
True ☐ **False** ☐

7 Danny thinks the food looks delicious.
True ☐ **False** ☐

Aa 1.6 FILL IN THE GAPS USING THE PHRASES IN THE PANEL

Good evening, Mr. Fisher. _____*How are you*_____ ?

1 I'm very _____ .

2 This _____ .

3 _____ , Mrs. Reid. How are you?

4 Hi, Sally. How _____ ?

5 I'm _____ you, Ms. Chopra.

6 May _____ Frank Hill?

7 I'm very pleased _____ , Diana.

8 _____ meet you, Holly.

are you doing

is Tim

well, thank you

~~How are you~~

Great to

to meet you

delighted to meet

I introduce

Good morning

💬 1.7 RESPOND TO THE GREETINGS, SPEAKING OUT LOUD

May I introduce Mr. Tom Grant?

> I'm ___*delighted*___ to meet you.

1 Hi, Vincent.

> _____ , Maria.

2 Hello, Mrs. Gardner. How are you?

> I'm very well, _____ .

3 This is Alexis.

> _____ to meet you.

4 Hi, Natasha. How are you doing?

> _____ , thanks.

5 Darren! Lovely to see you!

> Paul! _____ to see you, too.

Aa 2.1 COUNTRIES WRITE THE COUNTRY NAMES FROM THE PANEL UNDER THE CORRECT FLAGS

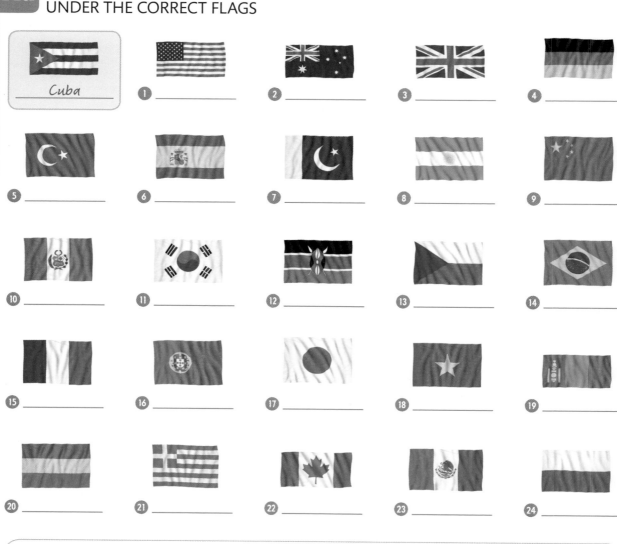

Cuba

1 _____

2 _____

3 _____

4 _____

5 _____

6 _____

7 _____

8 _____

9 _____

10 _____

11 _____

12 _____

13 _____

14 _____

15 _____

16 _____

17 _____

18 _____

19 _____

20 _____

21 _____

22 _____

23 _____

24 _____

Canada   Czech Republic   Poland   Germany   Turkey   Australia   Mexico   United Kingdom

Mongolia   Pakistan   United States of America   Argentina   South Korea   Spain   ~~Cuba~~

France   Peru   Bolivia   China   Portugal   Greece   Vietnam   Japan   Brazil   Kenya

03 Where things are

English uses prepositions to talk about where things are. It is important to learn the correct prepositions for different phrases describing locations and directions.

🔧 **New language** Prepositions of place
Aa Vocabulary Countries and nationalities
🧩 **New skill** Talking about where things are

🔧 3.1 CROSS OUT THE INCORRECT WORDS IN EACH SENTENCE

 Marge and Bert live in the Sunrise Apartments ~~on~~ / in / ~~opposite~~ the city center.

❶ There is a tree **to the left of** / **on** / **around** the tall building in town.

❷ We stayed in a small hotel just **in** / **around** / **by** the seaside.

❸ The town library is **opposite** / **right next to** / **across** the movie theater.

❹ Tom is planning on going for a walk **in** / **on** / **by** the country today.

❺ Norway and Australia are on **around** / **opposite** / **off** sides of the world.

❻  The Snow Slopes Ski Resort is **on** / **off** / **in** the mountains.

🔊

💬 3.2 USE THE CHART TO CREATE 10 SENTENCES AND SAY THEM OUT LOUD

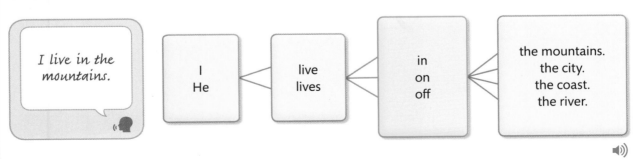

I live in the mountains.

| I / He | live / lives | in / on / off | the mountains. / the city. / the coast. / the river. |

🔊

3.3 LISTEN TO THE AUDIO AND ANSWER THE QUESTIONS

Jerry is a British student who recently moved to Spain.

Jerry is studying at Seville University.
True ☑ **False** ☐ **Not given** ☐

❶ Jerry is from a busy city in England.
True ☐ **False** ☐ **Not given** ☐

❷ In England he lived near the south coast.
True ☐ **False** ☐ **Not given** ☐

❸ Seville is on the Guadalquivir river.
True ☐ **False** ☐ **Not given** ☐

❹ Jerry is sharing an apartment with friends.
True ☐ **False** ☐ **Not given** ☐

❺ His apartment is on the river.
True ☐ **False** ☐ **Not given** ☐

❻ Next weekend he's touring Doñana National park.
True ☐ **False** ☐ **Not given** ☐

❼ The Doñana National park is in the mountains.
True ☐ **False** ☐ **Not given** ☐

3.4 FILL IN THE GAPS USING THE WORDS IN THE PANEL

The lighthouse is ___*on*___ the east coast.

❶ The castle is _____ the beach.

❷ The island is just _____ the coast.

❸ Visitors can take boat trips _____ the island.

❹ They can eat at the restaurant _____ the island.

❺ The statue is _____ the café and the church.

❻ The restaurant is _____ opposite the café.

❼ The lighthouse is diagonally _____ the church.

| right next to | | between | | off | | ~~on~~ |
| around | | on | | opposite | | directly |

3.5 MATCH THE BEGINNINGS OF THE SENTENCES TO THE CORRECT ENDINGS

They are traveling around

1 The lighthouse is just off

2 The park is diagonally

3 We stayed in a chalet in

4 There's a café right

5 Henry has a house by

6 It's halfway between

opposite the lake.

next to the theater.

the sea.

the world.

the airport and the hotel.

the coast.

the mountains.

3.6 READ THE WEB PAGE AND ANSWER THE QUESTIONS

Which country is Vancouver in?
America ☐ **Canada** ☑ **England** ☐

1 On which coast is Vancouver?
Atlantic ☐ **Indian** ☐ **Pacific** ☐

2 How close is the city to beaches?
Right next to ☐ **Far away** ☐ **Miles away** ☐

3 When did it host the Winter Olympics?
2008 ☐ **2010** ☐ **2012** ☐

4 How far away is Whistler?
10km ☐ **100km** ☐ **1,000km** ☐

5 What direction is Whistler from Vancouver?
South ☐ **East** ☐ **North** ☐

6 Where can you sail?
On the river ☐ **On the bay** ☐ **In the lake** ☐

Travel Time

HOME | ENTRIES | ABOUT | CONTACT

POSTED FRIDAY, AUGUST 28

Visit Vancouver

Vancouver is a popular tourist destination in Canada. It's right on the Pacific coast, so why not take a boat trip around the harbor? The city is right next to miles of beautiful beaches but it is also close to beautiful mountains. Vancouver hosted the Winter Olympics in 2010 and now has excellent transportation links to Whistler ski resort. Whistler is 100km north of Vancouver. When you visit Vancouver, you can ski in the mountains in the morning and sail on the bay in the afternoon! If you prefer to stay in the city, you can take a tour around Stanley Park or learn something new in Science World.

04 Numbers and statistics

Fractions, decimals, and percentages are all pronounced differently in spoken English, following a few simple rules.

⚙ **New language** Numbers in spoken English
Aa Vocabulary Sports events
🧩 **New skill** Using numbers in conversation

4.1 SAY THE NUMBERS OUT LOUD

⅕ → *one fifth*

1. 0.75 _____
2. 42% _____
3. ⅙ _____
4. 12.3 _____
5. ¾ _____

🔊

4.2 MATCH THE FIGURES TO THE CORRECT NUMBERS IN WORDS

⅗ → three fifths

1. 8.3
2. 79%
3. 2¼
4. 0.4
5. 15%
6. 1⅓

seventy-nine percent
zero point four
one and a third
three fifths
two and a quarter
eight point three
fifteen percent

🔊

4.3 LISTEN TO THE AUDIO AND WRITE ANSWERS TO THE QUESTIONS IN FULL SENTENCES

A sports commentator is providing the highlights of the Athletics Championship.

How full was the Stadium today?
The stadium was 90 percent full.

1. How high did Davis jump?
_____

2. By how much did Mwange beat the record?
_____

3. By how many seconds did Joslin win?
_____

4. What fraction of all medals does Canada hold?
_____

5. By how many centimeters did Edwards win?
_____

4.4 LISTEN TO THE AUDIO AND WRITE ALL THE NUMBERS AND STATISTICS YOU HEAR

A news reporter summarizes the results from an athletics tournament.

2.07

② _____ ④ _____ ⑥ _____

① _____ ③ _____ ⑤ _____ ⑦ _____

4.5 MARK THE STRESSED SYLLABLES AND SAY THE NUMBERS OUT LOUD

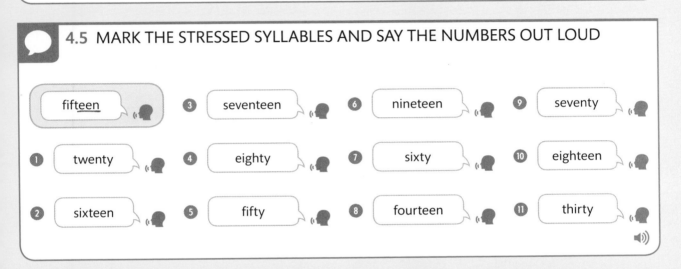

fif**teen**

③ seventeen

⑥ nineteen

⑨ seventy

① twenty

④ eighty

⑦ sixty

⑩ eighteen

② sixteen

⑤ fifty

⑧ fourteen

⑪ thirty

4.6 CROSS OUT THE MISSPELLED WORD IN EACH SENTENCE

The high jump bar is over ~~too~~ / **two** meters high.

① The Jamaican sprinter lost by **four fivths** / **four fifths** of a second.

② Tracey Livingstone won the race by **three twelvths** / **three twelfths** of a second.

③ The Russian contestant won by an **eighth** / **eigth** of an inch.

④ There were a total of **fourty** / **forty** runners in the marathon this year.

⑤ The American won the 100 meters back stroke by **five sixs** / **five sixths** of a second.

⑥ Maxwell Peterson came in **nineth** / **ninth** place out of 48 contestants.

21

05 Times and dates

There are many ways of saying the time and the date in English. American and British English speakers often use different forms.

⚙ **New language** Precise times
Aa Vocabulary Dates in US and UK English
New skill Talking about times and dates

5.1 SAY THE TIMES OUT LOUD

09:15 — *It's quarter past nine*

1 **10:30**

2 **11:45**

3 **12:00**

4 **14:50**

5 **15:24**

6 **17:14**

7 **19:37**

8 **21:48**

5.2 SAY THE DATES OUT LOUD

TIP
Remember the difference between UK and US dates.

09/05/01 (US)
September fifth, two thousand and one

1 **11/02/10 (UK)**

2 **03/04/12 (US)**

3 **09/23/06 (US)**

4 **31/12/14 (UK)**

5 **02/15/08 (US)**

5.3 MATCH THE TIMES TO THE STATEMENTS

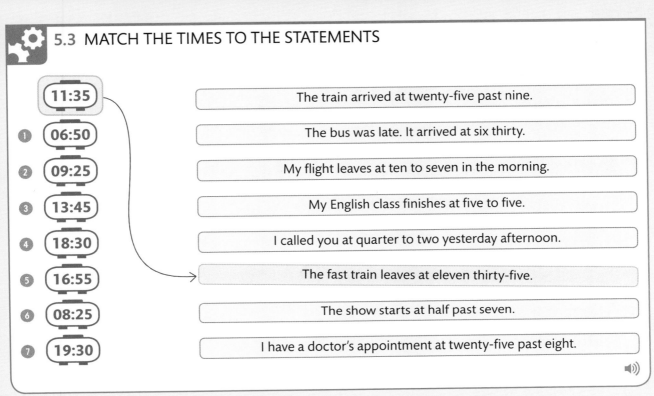

11:35	The train arrived at twenty-five past nine.
❶ **06:50**	The bus was late. It arrived at six thirty.
❷ **09:25**	My flight leaves at ten to seven in the morning.
❸ **13:45**	My English class finishes at five to five.
❹ **18:30**	I called you at quarter to two yesterday afternoon.
❺ **16:55**	The fast train leaves at eleven thirty-five.
❻ **08:25**	The show starts at half past seven.
❼ **19:30**	I have a doctor's appointment at twenty-five past eight.

5.4 LISTEN TO THE AUDIO AND ANSWER THE QUESTIONS

People are talking about important dates and times in their lives.

Tim and Alison got married on...
February 10, 2004 ☐
August 6, 2009 ☑
November 30, 2015 ☐

❶ Simon's flight leaves at...
10:30 ☐
15:10 ☐
14:50 ☐

❷ Jamie graduated from college on...
June 30 ☐
June 13 ☐
July 30 ☐

❸ The fast train to Edinburgh leaves at...
07:24 ☐
11:24 ☐
10:45 ☐

❹ Harry's grandfather's 80th birthday was on...
October 27 ☐
November 27 ☐
November 17 ☐

❺ Jane and Paul's wedding is at...
2:30pm ☐
3:30pm ☐
4:30pm ☐

Contact details

Telephone numbers, street addresses, email addresses, and web addresses are expressed in slightly different ways in US and UK English.

✿ **New language** Letters and numbers
Aa Vocabulary Contact details
✦ **New skill** Exchanging personal information

6.1 LISTEN TO THE AUDIO AND WRITE THE PLACE NAMES THAT ARE SPELLED OUT

Shanghai

1 _____

2 _____

3 _____

4 _____

5 _____

6 _____

7 _____

8 _____

9 _____

10 _____

6.2 ANSWER THE QUESTIONS BY SPELLING THE WORDS OUT LOUD

How do you spell "Durban?"

D-U-R-B-A-N

1 How do you spell "California?"

2 How do you spell "Paddington?"

3 How do you spell "Bloomfield?"

4 How do you spell "Birmingham?"

5 How do you spell "Hong Kong?"

6 How do you spell "Cambridge?"

7 How do you spell "Sydney?"

8 How do you spell "New Delhi?"

6.3 LISTEN TO THE AUDIO AND WRITE DOWN THE PHONE NUMBERS YOU HEAR

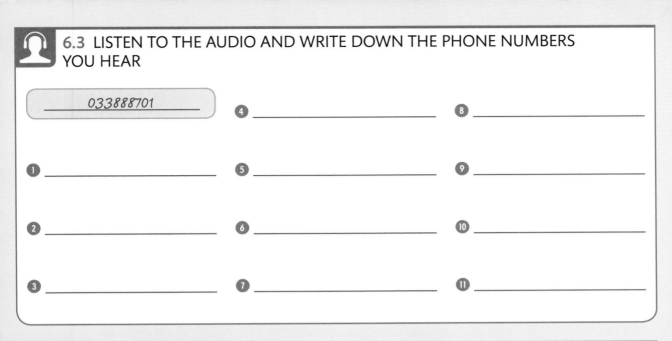

033888701

1 _____

2 _____

3 _____

4 _____

5 _____

6 _____

7 _____

8 _____

9 _____

10 _____

11 _____

6.4 LOOK AT THE ADDRESS BOOK ENTRY AND RESPOND TO THE AUDIO, SPEAKING OUT LOUD

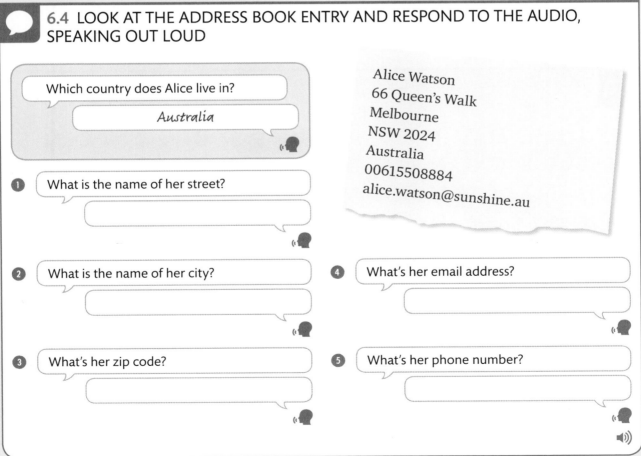

Which country does Alice live in?

Australia

Alice Watson
66 Queen's Walk
Melbourne
NSW 2024
Australia
00615508884
alice.watson@sunshine.au

1 What is the name of her street?

2 What is the name of her city?

3 What's her zip code?

4 What's her email address?

5 What's her phone number?

6.5 LOOK AT THE BUSINESS CARD AND WRITE ANSWERS TO THE QUESTIONS AS FULL SENTENCES

> Who does this business card belong to?
> _It belongs to Rachel Brodie._

1 What is her surname?

_____

2 What's her job?

_____

3 Which company does she work at?

_____

4 What's her phone number?

_____

RACHEL BRODIE
Sales Manager

Trademark Printers Ltd.

Mobile: 0785 9044678
Email: rachel.brodie@trademark.com

5 What's her email address?

_____

Aa 6.6 FIND NINE WORDS FOR CONTACT DETAILS IN THE GRID

```
P G N C D S T R E E T N S D R A O W O N S
H S A X O I N G T S E F T I T L E Q E N V
O D E T J U M D S M T R I I S E M A I L D
N I N O E R N I U T C A I R R T I T C U I
E K A W E B X T R D I N T X S S A D I N Z
N D I N R Y A D R A E X D E Y T N X E N I
U Z L E L A O Z I Y R I Z L A O N O R I P
M A V H S N V O N S T N D S N V O A X N C
B C D J T N D E G J A G I T N D E J M M O
E H I E A R I A I E O S S A R I A E O E D
R E C B H O U S E N U M B E R K I B G Z E
```